COMMENTARY P

MASTERING THE ART OF
ENGAGING FOOTBALL ANALYSIS

ANGELA KEEN

DISCLAIMER

The information provided in this book, "Commentary Playbook: Mastering the Art of Engaging Football Analysis," is for general informational purposes only. The author, Angela Keen, makes no representations or warranties of any kind, express or implied, about the completeness, accuracy, reliability, suitability, or availability concerning the content contained within.

Any reliance you place on the information provided in this book is strictly at your own risk. The author will not be liable for any losses or damages arising from the use of this book.

The techniques, strategies, and opinions expressed in this book are based on the author's experiences and research up to the copyright date and are subject to change. Readers are encouraged to conduct their own further research and seek professional advice if needed.

TABLE OF CONTENT

INTRODUCTION

Welcome to "Commentary Playbook: Mastering the Art of Engaging Football Analysis" by Angela Keen. I am thrilled to invite you into the exciting world of football commentary and share valuable insights on mastering the art of delivering compelling and insightful analysis.

As an author deeply passionate about both football and effective communication, I have crafted this playbook to serve as your guide in elevating your understanding of the game and refining your skills as a commentator. Whether you're an aspiring sports broadcaster, a seasoned commentator, or simply a football enthusiast, this book aims to provide you with a comprehensive toolkit to enhance your commentary prowess.

Inside these pages, you'll discover a blend of strategic techniques, practical tips, and anecdotes from the exciting realm of football commentary.

From dissecting key plays to capturing the essence of the game, I've curated a resource that goes beyond the basics, offering a deep dive into the nuances that make commentary truly engaging.

Feel free to explore the chapters at your own pace, as each section is designed to build upon the last, culminating in a holistic understanding of the art of football analysis. Whether you're looking to kickstart a career in sports broadcasting or simply wish to enhance your enjoyment of the game, "Commentary Playbook" is here to empower you.

Thank you for embarking on this journey with me. I hope this playbook becomes a valuable companion in your pursuit of mastering the craft of football commentary. Let's dive into the exhilarating world of analyzing the beautiful game together!

CHAPTER ONE

THE ESSENCE OF COMMENTARY

In the captivating realm of sports, where the roar of the crowd mingles with the unmistakable rhythm of a bouncing ball, few elements weave the magic of the game quite like commentary. It is a symphony of words, a dance of narratives that transcends the boundaries of the playing field. As a writer, let us embark on a journey to unravel the essence of commentary, exploring its profound impact on our perception of the beautiful game.

At its core, commentary is more than a mere description of events on the pitch. It is the invisible hand that guides spectators through the intricate tapestry of the game, transforming a series of actions into a compelling story. Every phrase uttered by the commentator is a brushstroke, painting vivid images in the minds of those who witness the spectacle. It is an art form, and like any masterpiece, it requires skill, passion, and a deep understanding of the subject.

One cannot discuss the essence of commentary without acknowledging its power to shape our emotional connection to the game.

The right words, delivered with precision and emotion, have the ability to elevate a routine play into a moment etched in the collective memory of fans. The commentator becomes a storyteller, breathing life into the game, turning it into a shared experience that transcends borders and cultures.

In the intricacies of football, commentary is the bridge that connects the seasoned fanatic to the casual observer. It provides context, demystifying the complexities of strategies and tactics. A well-crafted commentary educates, offering insights into the nuances that escape the untrained eye. It transforms the mundane into the extraordinary, revealing the poetry in the players' movements and the strategic brilliance of the coaches.

The essence of commentary lies not only in the words spoken but in the spaces between them. It is the pregnant pause before a penalty kick, the hushed anticipation as the ball hangs in the air, and the explosion of emotion when it hits the back of the net.

A skilled commentator understands the ebb and flow of the game, using silence as a canvas to amplify the drama, allowing the audience to savor the tension and celebrate the release.

As we delve deeper, we uncover the responsibility that comes with the art of commentary. It is a delicate balance of objectivity and passion, a dance between unbiased analysis and unbridled enthusiasm. A commentator, in essence, is a custodian of the game's spirit, entrusted with the task of preserving its integrity while igniting the flames of passion in the hearts of the audience.

The essence of commentary is a rich tapestry woven from the threads of language, emotion, and expertise. It is a living, breathing entity that transforms the game from a physical spectacle into a shared narrative.

As a writer and a lover of the game, I invite you to appreciate the nuances of commentary, to savor the words that echo through stadiums and living rooms alike, and to recognize the profound impact they have on our experience of football – the beautiful game that transcends boundaries and unites us in a collective celebration of skill, strategy, and sheer human brilliance.

UNDERSTANDING THE ROLE OF A FOOTBALL COMMENTATOR

In the electrifying world of football, where every pass, tackle, and goal carry the weight of a thousand emotions, there exists a silent orchestrator – the football commentator. Beyond the echoes of the crowd and the thunderous applause, the commentator weaves a narrative that transcends the boundaries of the pitch. Join me in exploring the multifaceted role of a football commentator, delving into the intricacies that make this profession both an art and a science.

At first glance, a football commentator may seem like a mere voice on the airwaves, providing a play-by-play account of the game. However, their role extends far beyond that of a detached observer. A skilled commentator is a storyteller, transforming the dynamics of the game into a captivating narrative that engages and enchants audiences worldwide.

The commentator is, in essence, the bridge between the players on the field and the millions of passionate fans around the globe.

It is a role that demands not only a deep understanding of the game's technical aspects but also an acute awareness of the emotional currents that run through the stadium. The commentator must decipher the unspoken language of the game, translating the intricacies of tactics and strategies into a digestible and compelling tale for viewers.

One cannot overlook the educator's hat that the football commentator wears with pride. Beyond the thrill of the moment, these individuals are responsible for providing insights into the sport's finer nuances. Whether explaining the significance of a tactical change or breaking down the biomechanics of a breathtaking goal, the commentator serves as a trusted guide, enhancing the viewer's understanding and appreciation of the game.

Yet, the role is not without its challenges. A football commentator must navigate the delicate balance between passion and objectivity. While enthusiasm adds flavor to the commentary, it is crucial to maintain a fair and unbiased perspective.

Negotiating this tightrope requires finesse, as the commentator walks the fine line between celebrating the sport's brilliance and offering constructive criticism when warranted.

In the age of global connectivity, football has become a universal language, spoken and understood by people from diverse cultures and backgrounds. The football commentator, therefore, holds a position of cultural significance. Their words resonate not only with local fans but also with those tuning in from different corners of the world. As a result, a commentator must be mindful of the impact of their words, fostering a sense of inclusivity and unity among a diverse audience.

Understanding the role of a football commentator is akin to unraveling the layers of a complex and nuanced performance. It is a dance of words, emotions, and expertise that transforms a mere sports event into a shared experience.

As we sit back to enjoy the next match, let us not merely hear the commentator's voice but appreciate the artistry behind it — a crucial component that enriches our connection to the beautiful game.

THE IMPACT OF COMMENTARY ON AUDIENCE ENGAGEMENT

The commentator's voice resonates, shaping our experience of the game. Join me in unraveling the profound impact of commentary on audience engagement, exploring the symbiotic relationship between the spoken word and the collective heartbeat of sports enthusiasts.

At its core, commentary serves as the emotional soundtrack of a sporting event. The commentator's voice is the conduit through which the drama, excitement, and narratives of the game reach our ears. It transforms a sequence of actions into a riveting story, creating a connection between the audience and the unfolding spectacle on the field. The commentator is not just an observer; they are the maestro, orchestrating our emotional journey through the highs and lows of the game.

One cannot underestimate the role of commentary in providing context and understanding.

As the ball moves across the pitch and players execute strategic maneuvers, the commentator decodes the game's intricacies for the audience. Whether it's unraveling tactical brilliance, explaining the significance of a critical play, or highlighting a player's exceptional skill, commentary elevates our comprehension, turning casual viewers into informed enthusiasts.

The commentator's influence extends beyond the realm of analysis; it fosters a sense of camaraderie among fans. A well-crafted commentary creates a shared experience, transforming a solitary act of watching into a communal celebration. It forges a bond among supporters, regardless of geographical distances or team loyalties, as they collectively ride the emotional rollercoaster shaped by the commentator's words.

Moreover, the commentator is a conduit for passion and enthusiasm. Their energy is contagious, infusing the broadcast with a fervor that reverberates through the screen.

The right turn of phrase, the well-timed crescendo of excitement, or the poignant pause can elevate the viewing experience, turning a routine match into an unforgettable moment etched in the memories of the audience.

In the digital age, where social media amplifies every aspect of the sporting experience, commentary becomes a focal point of conversation. Memorable quotes, witty observations, and emotional reactions from commentators become shared currency among fans, creating a vibrant online community that extends the conversation beyond the final whistle.

As you settle in to enjoy the next game, take a moment to appreciate the unseen architect of your experience—the commentator. Their words, delivered with passion and precision, shape the way we perceive, understand, and connect with the game we love. In the symphony of sports, the commentator's voice is a vital instrument, harmonizing with the cheers of the crowd to create a timeless melody of shared emotion.

CHAPTER TWO

FOUNDATIONS OF FOOTBALL KNOWLEDGE

Beyond the dazzling skills of players and the thunderous cheers of the crowd lies a world of nuances and intricacies that form the foundations of football knowledge. Join me as we delve into the essential elements that shape our understanding of the beautiful game, exploring the rich tapestry that underlies the spectacle on the pitch.

At its core, football knowledge is built upon a solid understanding of the game's fundamental principles. From the dimensions of the pitch to the rules that govern play, these foundational elements provide the scaffolding upon which our appreciation of football rests. Understanding the offside rule, the significance of a corner kick, or the role of a free-kick adds layers of comprehension, transforming a casual observer into an informed enthusiast.

The anatomy of a football team is another cornerstone of knowledge. Beyond recognizing star players, understanding the various positions and their roles on the field is crucial.

From the goalkeeper as the last line of defense to the strikers aiming for the back of the net, each position contributes to the intricate dance of strategy and skill that defines the sport.

Tactics and strategies form the strategic bedrock of football knowledge. Recognizing different formations, understanding the purpose of pressing, and deciphering counter-attacks all contribute to a deeper appreciation of the game. It's a chess match on grass, where managers meticulously plan and execute their moves, and football knowledge allows us to decode the brilliance behind each play.

Skill appreciation is another vital aspect of football knowledge. Whether it's marveling at a perfectly executed bicycle kick, the finesse of a well-placed pass, or the agility of a goalkeeper's save, recognizing and appreciating the diverse skills showcased by players enhances our enjoyment of the game. Football becomes not just a competition but a showcase of human athleticism and creativity.

Football's rich history and its impact on cultures worldwide add a layer of cultural understanding to the foundations of football knowledge. From legendary players who shaped eras to iconic moments that transcend time, delving into the historical tapestry of the sport connects us to its roots and deepens our sense of belonging to a global football community.

The foundations of football knowledge extend beyond the pitch to the broader context of the sport's impact on society. Understanding the social, economic, and cultural dimensions of football adds depth to our perception. Football is not just a game; it's a cultural phenomenon that influences identities, fosters unity, and serves as a canvas for storytelling on a global scale.

The foundations of football knowledge are a multidimensional exploration that goes beyond the surface spectacle of the game. It's a journey that involves understanding the rules, appreciating the skills, decoding strategies, and embracing the cultural significance of football.

As you embark on this exploration, may your love for the beautiful game deepen, and may your understanding of its intricacies enrich your experience as a devoted enthusiast.

MASTERING THE BASICS: RULES AND REGULATIONS

Join me on a journey to master the basics, to understand the code that governs the world's most beloved sport, and to appreciate the intricate dance that unfolds on the pitch within the confines of these regulations.

At the heart of any sport is a set of rules that provides structure, fairness, and a level playing field. Football, with its global appeal, has a set of regulations that serves as the guiding framework for players, officials, and spectators alike. Understanding these rules is not merely a formality; it is the gateway to a deeper appreciation of the sport.

The dimensions of the pitch, the markings, and the placement of the goalposts are the architectural elements that set the stage for the drama. Mastering these basics is akin to understanding the canvas upon which the art of football is painted. The pitch becomes a theater where every pass, every goal, and every tackle unfold within the defined boundaries, creating a space where the magic of the game comes to life.

The offside rule, often a source of confusion and animated debates, is a fundamental aspect that shapes the ebb and flow of play. Grasping the intricacies of this rule allows spectators to decipher the strategic nuances employed by teams. It transforms the seemingly chaotic movements on the field into a strategic ballet, where players position themselves with precision to exploit or defend against the offside trap.

Fouls and free kicks are the regulatory checkpoints that maintain order and fairness. Understanding the types of fouls, the consequences they entail, and the positioning of the ball for free kicks adds layers to our comprehension. It is not just about penalizing misconduct; it is about restoring balance and ensuring that the game remains a contest of skill rather than a battle of physicality.

Yellow and red cards, often brandished by referees, are more than cautionary signals. They are the guardians of sportsmanship and fair play. Mastering the consequences of these disciplinary actions is essential in appreciating the importance of maintaining the integrity of the game.

It's a delicate balance between intensity and respect that players must navigate, and spectators must comprehend.

The concept of stoppage time, an extension of play beyond the regulation 90 minutes, is another dimension of football's temporal dance. Injury time, added by the referee, can be a source of last-minute drama, turning the tide of a match in the dying moments. Understanding this element adds an element of anticipation, reminding us that the game's fate can change in an instant.

Mastering the basics of rules and regulations in football is not a chore; it is an invitation to delve deeper into the beauty and complexity of the sport. It is the key to unlocking the secrets that lie within the seemingly simple act of kicking a ball. As you watch the next match, may your understanding of the rules elevate your enjoyment, turning each goal, each pass, and each decision into a chapter in the thrilling narrative of football.

KEY ELEMENTS OF THE GAME: PLAYERS, POSITIONS, AND STRATEGIES

In the grand theater of football, where skillful players move in orchestrated harmony, and strategic brilliance unfolds with every pass, the key elements of the game lay the foundation for the beautiful spectacle we witness on the pitch. Join me in unraveling the intricate tapestry of players, positions, and strategies, exploring the dynamic elements that transform a simple game into a mesmerizing ballet of athleticism and tactics.

Players: The Heartbeat of the Game

At the epicenter of football are the players, the artists who breathe life into the sport. From agile goalkeepers to fleet-footed forwards, each player contributes a unique skill set to the collective symphony of the team. Understanding the players and their roles is akin to recognizing the cast in a theatrical production, each with a distinct part to play in the unfolding drama.

Goalkeepers, the custodians of the net, are the first line of defense, displaying acrobatics and reflexes that defy belief.

Defenders act as the fortresses, thwarting opposition attacks and ensuring the safety of their goal. Midfielders orchestrate the rhythm, linking defense to attack with vision and precision. Forwards, the goal-hungry maestros, provide the crescendo, turning strategy into tangible results on the scoreboard.

Positions: The Chessboard of Strategy

The strategic chessboard of football is defined by player positions. From the iconic number 10 orchestrating the playmaker role to the tireless full-backs patrolling the flanks, each position has a specific purpose. Understanding these roles is like deciphering the tactical language spoken by coaches and players, unraveling the intricate formations that dictate the ebb and flow of the game.

Strikers, the goal-hunters, position themselves strategically to exploit defensive weaknesses. Midfielders, the engines of the team, balance offensive and defensive duties, ensuring a seamless transition between phases of play. Defenders, the sentinels, hold the fort and initiate attacks from the back.

The goalkeeper, the last line of defense, is the anchor that safeguards the team's fortunes.

Strategies: The Tactical Chess Match

Football is a strategic chess match played on a green battlefield. Coaches meticulously devise strategies that exploit opponents' vulnerabilities while shoring up their own defenses. Formations like 4-3-3, 4-4-2, or the adventurous 3-5-2 are not mere numbers; they are blueprints that shape the team's approach to the game.

Understanding defensive strategies, such as high-pressing or zonal marking, illuminates the art of regaining possession. Offensive tactics, like tiki-taka or the long-ball approach, showcase the diversity of styles that teams employ to break down defenses. Counter-attacks, set-pieces, and positional play are elements of a grand tactical symphony orchestrated by managers who aim to outwit their counterparts.

The Harmonious Ballet of Football

The key elements of players, positions, and strategies are the notes and movements that compose the harmonious ballet of football. Every match is a performance, and each player is a dancer, contributing their skill, flair, and strategic prowess to the collective masterpiece. As you immerse yourself in the next match, may your understanding of these key elements enrich your appreciation, turning each kick, each run, and each strategic maneuver into a chapter in the captivating narrative of the beautiful game.

CHAPTER THREE

CRAFTING COMPELLING NARRATIVES

The role of narrative in sports commentary goes beyond a mere recitation of events on the pitch. It is a transformative force that turns a sequence of actions into a captivating story, weaving together the highs and lows, the triumphs and setbacks, into a narrative tapestry that resonates with audiences. The commentator, in this context, becomes a storyteller, shaping the way we perceive and emotionally connect with the unfolding drama.

Crafting a compelling narrative in sports involves constructing a storyline that unfolds over the course of a match. It is about capturing the essence of the game's narrative arc, from the anticipation of the kickoff to the climax at the final whistle. A well-crafted narrative engages the audience, guiding them through the twists and turns of the match, creating a sense of suspense, excitement, and emotional investment.

The characters in the sports narrative are the players, each with a unique story to tell.

Understanding their histories, personal journeys, and on-field rivalries adds depth to the narrative. Player profiles, historical context, and personal anecdotes enrich the storytelling experience, providing the audience with a more profound connection to the individuals who bring the narrative to life.

The tone of a sports narrative is as crucial as the words themselves. It is the emotional pitch that sets the atmosphere for the story. Whether conveying the thrill of a last-minute goal or the disappointment of a missed opportunity, the tone shapes the audience's emotional response. Crafting the right tone involves a delicate balance between excitement, empathy, and impartiality, ensuring a nuanced and authentic storytelling experience.

The art of sports commentary lies not just in what is said but how it is said. Wordplay, eloquence, and the strategic use of language enhance the narrative's beauty.

A well-turned phrase, a clever metaphor, or a poetic description can elevate the commentary from a mere account of events to a literary experience, making the audience feel the poetry in the players' movements and the drama in every pass.

Crafting compelling narratives in sports is an art that transforms the ephemeral moments on the field into enduring stories. The commentator's role as a storyteller is not merely to inform but to immerse the audience in the emotional landscape of the game. As you listen to the next sports commentary, may you appreciate the craftsmanship behind the words, recognizing that the true beauty of sports lies not just in the game itself but in the stories woven around it.

STORYTELLING TECHNIQUES IN FOOTBALL COMMENTARY

Every great story begins with context, and football commentary is no exception. Before the first whistle blows, a skilled commentator sets the stage by delving into the historical context, team dynamics, and the stakes involved. By providing the audience with a narrative backdrop, the commentator builds anticipation and invests the viewers emotionally in the unfolding drama.

Example: *"As these two historic rivals meet on the pitch, memories of their last clash linger in the air. The stakes are high, with both teams vying for a coveted spot in the finals. This is not just a game; it's a chapter in a long-standing football saga."*

Character Development

In football, the players are the protagonists, each with a unique story to tell. Commentators use character development techniques to humanize players, sharing anecdotes, personal histories, and moments of triumph or adversity.

By weaving these narratives into the commentary, a connection is forged between the audience and the players, making the match a personal and emotional journey.

Example: *"Watch closely as the young striker takes the field today. Born in the heart of the city, he carries the dreams of the local fans on his shoulders. His journey from the youth academy to this pivotal moment is a testament to dedication and talent."*

Building Tension and Climax

A compelling story thrives on tension and climax, and football commentary mirrors this narrative structure. Skilled commentators build suspense as the game unfolds, heightening the emotional stakes with strategic pauses, tone modulation, and word choice. The climax, whether a last-minute goal or a crucial penalty, becomes the pinnacle of the narrative, leaving an indelible mark on the audience.

Example: *"The clock is ticking down, and the tension in the stadium is palpable.*

As the captain lines up for the free-kick just outside the box, the crowd holds its breath. This could be the moment that defines the entire season."

Fluid Transition between Scenes

In storytelling, fluid transitions are essential for a seamless narrative flow. Similarly, in football commentary, the ability to smoothly transition between different phases of the game is crucial. Whether shifting from an intense goal-scoring opportunity to a defensive maneuver, a skilled commentator ensures that the transitions are natural, maintaining the coherence of the overarching story.

Example: *"From the jubilation of that incredible goal to the defensive resilience displayed in the following minutes, the narrative of this match is evolving rapidly. The ebb and flow of emotions make this game a rollercoaster of storytelling on the pitch."*

Reflecting on the Story's Arc

As the final whistle blows, a masterful storyteller in football commentary reflects on the arc of the narrative.

Summing up the key moments, acknowledging standout performances, and contextualizing the match within the broader season or tournament contribute to a satisfying conclusion. This reflection leaves the audience with a sense of closure and a deeper understanding of the ongoing storylines in the world of football.

Example: *"What a match we've witnessed today. The twists and turns, the highs and lows – they all contribute to the grand narrative of this football season. As the players leave the pitch, we are left to contemplate the impact of this chapter in the unfolding story of the beautiful game."*

Storytelling techniques in football commentary are the brushstrokes that paint the canvas of a match. As you immerse yourself in the next game, listen not just to the commentary but to the narrative being woven— the tales of triumph, the sagas of resilience, and the stories that make football more than just a game but a compelling journey of human drama.

LEVERAGING HISTORICAL CONTEXT FOR ENHANCED ANALYSIS

One of the most potent benefits of historical context in football analysis is the ability to unveil patterns and trends. Teams often exhibit recurring strategies, styles, or tendencies that can be traced back through seasons. By recognizing these patterns, analysts can make more informed predictions, anticipate tactical approaches, and understand the evolution of a team's playing identity.

Example: "*Looking back at their previous encounters, we notice a recurring pattern of the team favoring a possession-based strategy against similar opponents. This historical context provides a valuable clue about their likely approach in today's crucial match.*"

The history of head-to-head matchups between teams offers a treasure trove of information.

Examining past encounters provides valuable context for understanding the dynamics of the rivalry, the psychological aspects of player matchups, and the impact of historical results on the current state of affairs. This knowledge becomes a strategic asset in predicting outcomes and assessing the stakes in pivotal fixtures.

Example: "*In the last five meetings between these two teams, we've observed a consistent struggle for dominance in the midfield. Today's battle in the center of the park is a continuation of this historical struggle for control and influence.*"

The historical trajectory of individual players adds depth to the analysis. Tracking a player's performance over multiple seasons reveals trends in form, consistency, and adaptability. Historical context allows analysts to assess how players have evolved, understand their strengths and weaknesses, and predict how they might influence the outcome of a current match based on their historical performances.

Example: "This seasoned striker has consistently excelled against teams with a high defensive line.

His historical prowess in exploiting such situations suggests that today's opponents might face a challenging task in containing him."

Managers play a pivotal role in shaping a team's identity and success. Analyzing a manager's historical track record, including past achievements, preferred tactical approaches, and performance in specific situations, provides crucial context for assessing their impact on the current team. This insight helps in understanding the overall philosophy and direction a team is likely to take under a particular managerial helm.

Example: "The new manager's historical tendency to prioritize attacking full-backs is evident in the team's recent performances. This strategic shift reflects the influence of the manager's proven tactical approach from previous stints."

Every team has its historical milestones—memorable victories, significant defeats, and breakthrough moments. Leveraging these historical milestones in analysis provides a cultural and emotional backdrop to a team's journey.

Understanding the impact of past milestones on the team's morale, fanbase, and overall confidence contributes to a holistic analysis that goes beyond statistics.

Example: *"The last time these two teams met on this ground; it marked a historic comeback for the home side. The emotional resonance of that victory may influence the team's mindset and determination in today's crucial fixture."*

Leveraging historical context in football analysis is akin to flipping through the pages of a richly woven novel. It provides depth, perspective, and a narrative backdrop that enhances the understanding of the present. As you delve into the next match analysis, may the echoes of the past guide you in unraveling the intricate stories that shape the ever-evolving drama of football.

CHAPTER FOUR

BUILDING A UNIQUE COMMENTARY STYLE

Your authenticity is your greatest asset. Building a unique commentary style begins with embracing your own voice, personality, and perspective. Don't shy away from injecting elements of your true self into your commentary. Whether it's your enthusiasm, humor, or personal anecdotes, authenticity establishes a genuine connection with your audience.

Example: *"Bringing you the action from the heart of the stadium, I'm not just a commentator; I'm a fellow fan sharing in the excitement of the beautiful game with you."*

Commentary is not just about the words; it's about the rhythm and cadence of your delivery. Experiment with pacing, modulate your tone, and discover the rhythm that feels most natural to you. Your unique rhythm adds a musicality to your commentary, making it engaging and memorable for your audience.

Example: "*As the tension builds on the pitch, allow the tempo of my voice to mirror the heartbeat of the game, capturing every rise and fall of emotion.*"

A signature phrase or catchphrase can become your calling card, instantly recognizable to your audience. Whether it's a clever turn of phrase, a motivational tagline, or a unique way of describing key moments, a well-crafted catchphrase adds flair and personality to your commentary.

Example: "*And there it is, folks! A goal that echoes through the annals of football history. Talk about turning dreams into reality!*"

Adaptability is key. Tailor your commentary style to the nature of the game, the teams involved, and the emotions at play. Whether it's injecting humor into a lighthearted match or adopting a more serious tone for a high-stakes fixture, a versatile commentator can navigate different scenarios while maintaining a consistent personal touch.

Example: "*In this heated derby, the banter is as fierce as the tackles. Let's bring some humor to the* intensity and celebrate the spirit of rivalry on the pitch."

Building a unique commentary style involves creating a connection with your audience.

Acknowledge the comments and sentiments of your viewers, engage with them on social media, and make them feel like they are part of the conversation. A commentator who listens and responds builds a community around their unique style.

Example: "*Shoutout to all our viewers chiming in from around the world. Your passion fuels the energy of our commentary, making this a shared experience for football lovers everywhere.*

Evolution is inherent in the process of building a unique commentary style. Continuously refine and adapt your style based on feedback, experiences, and personal growth. Embrace the journey of self-discovery within your commentary, always striving to enhance and elevate your unique voice.

Example: "*Just like the players on the field, my commentary style is a work in progress. Let's embark on this journey together, discovering new dimensions and enhancing the way we experience the game."*

Building a unique commentary style is an art form that requires authenticity, adaptability, and a deep connection with your audience.

As you embark on this exciting endeavor, remember that your voice in the world of sports commentary is not just a commentary—it's a story waiting to be told uniquely by you.

DEVELOPING YOUR VOICE: TONE, PACE, AND INFLECTION

Tone is the musicality of your commentary, the emotional undertone that colors your words. Experiment with different tones—whether it's the excitement of a goal, the empathy during a player's struggle, or the analysis of a tactical move. Your tone sets the mood, shaping the atmosphere of the match for your listeners.

Example: "*A sublime goal! The excitement in my voice mirrors the electric energy in the stadium, capturing the sheer brilliance of that moment.*"

Pace is the heartbeat of your commentary. Play with the tempo, adjusting it to match the cadence of the game. Speed up during moments of intensity, slow down for strategic analysis, and find the rhythm that mirrors the ebb and flow of the match. Your pace dictates the pulse of the commentary, guiding your audience through the peaks and valleys of the game.

Example: *"Hold your breath, folks! We're entering a crucial phase of the match, and the pace of my commentary mirrors the heart-pounding suspense on the pitch."*

Inflection is the emphasis you place on certain words or phrases, adding color and emphasis to your commentary. Master the art of inflection to highlight key moments, express excitement, or convey nuanced insights. Your inflection becomes the brushstroke that paints vivid images in the minds of your listeners.

Example: *"And he scores! The inflection in my voice captures the crescendo of emotion, emphasizing the magnitude of that goal and the impact it has on the match."*

Just as a skilled musician adjusts their performance to suit the mood of a composition, a commentator tailors their style to the emotional landscape of the game. Whether it's injecting energy into a lively match or adopting a more reflective tone during strategic pauses, your ability to match your commentary style to the prevailing mood enhances the overall experience for your audience.

Example: "*In this friendly encounter, the mood is light, and my commentary follows suit. Let's bring some humor and camaraderie to the airwaves as we enjoy the beautiful game together.*"

Developing your voice is a quest for authenticity in expression. Allow your personality to shine through your commentary. Whether you're naturally exuberant, composed, witty, or analytical, embrace your authentic self. Your genuine expression becomes the anchor that fosters a deeper connection with your audience.

Example: "*I can't contain my excitement as we witness this breathtaking play! Authenticity in my expression is the key to sharing the sheer joy of the game with you.*"

The art of developing your voice is an ongoing exploration and refinement. Listen to your own commentary, seek feedback, and be open to evolution. As you refine your tone, pace, and inflection, you carve a unique sonic path that distinguishes your voice in the world of sports commentary.

Example: "*Every match is an opportunity to refine my commentary style. Join me in this continuous exploration, where each game becomes a canvas for refining the brushstrokes of my sonic signature.*"

Developing your voice in commentary is an art that involves mastering the nuances of tone, pace, and inflection. As you embark on this sonic journey, may your commentary become not just a narration of the game but a distinctive melody that resonates with the hearts of your audience.

BALANCING ENTHUSIASM AND OBJECTIVITY

Enthusiasm is the heartbeat of sports commentary. It is the infectious energy that transforms a routine play into a moment of brilliance and elevates a goal into a symphony of celebration. Embracing enthusiasm allows a commentator to share the excitement of the game, creating a dynamic and vibrant atmosphere for the audience.

Example: *"What a phenomenal strike! The enthusiasm in my voice mirrors the sheer joy on the pitch, capturing the raw emotion of that stunning goal."*

Objectivity is the anchor that grounds commentary in fairness and accuracy. It involves maintaining a neutral stance, free from biases or personal affiliations. Objectivity allows a commentator to provide insightful analysis, acknowledging the strengths and weaknesses of all teams and players, regardless of personal preferences.

Example: "*While the home team is putting on a commendable performance, it's essential to recognize the strategic brilliance displayed by the visiting side. Objectivity ensures a fair assessment of both teams.*"

Balancing enthusiasm and objectivity involve seamless transitions between moments of celebration and moments of analysis. A skilled commentator navigates the shifts with finesse, ensuring that the emotional highs do not compromise the clarity and fairness of the commentary. This creates a cohesive and engaging narrative that resonates with a diverse audience.

Example: "*A fantastic goal there! Now, let's take a step back and analyze the defensive lapses that led to that breakthrough. Balancing the highs with insightful analysis is the key to a well-rounded commentary.*"

Enthusiasm doesn't negate the ability to acknowledge excellence, even from opposing teams. Objectivity encourages a commentator to celebrate outstanding performances and moments of brilliance, regardless of team allegiances. This acknowledgment adds credibility to the commentary and fosters a sense of respect among fans.

Example: "*Although it's the rival team, we can't help but applaud the remarkable save by their goalkeeper. Objectivity requires us to recognize excellence wherever we see it on the pitch.*"

Striking the balance between enthusiasm and objectivity requires a willingness to accept constructive criticism. Feedback from viewers and peers provides valuable insights into maintaining a fair and engaging commentary style. Embracing criticism with humility fosters growth and ensures a continuous refinement of one's approach.

Example: "*Your feedback is invaluable in refining our commentary. Let's work together to strike the right balance, ensuring an enjoyable experience for fans of all teams.*"

Ultimately, the success of balancing enthusiasm and objectivity lies in connecting with the audience. Understanding the diverse perspectives of viewers and catering to a broad spectrum of football enthusiasts ensures that the commentary resonates with a wide audience.

Building this connection adds depth to the commentary, transforming it into a shared experience for fans worldwide.

Example: "*Our audience spans across different teams and regions. By balancing enthusiasm and objectivity, we aim to create a commentary that speaks to the passion of every football lover, regardless of their allegiance.*"

The art of commentary is a delicate dance, where enthusiasm and objectivity twirl in harmony. As you immerse yourself in the next match, may the commentary strike the perfect balance, amplifying the joy of the game while offering insightful perspectives that enrich the overall experience.

CHAPTER FIVE

STRATEGIC ANALYSIS IN PLAY-BY-PLAY

Play-by-play commentary begins with decoding the formations and tactical systems employed by teams. Recognizing the strategic setup, whether it's a classic 4-4-2 or an adventurous 3-5-2, sets the stage for understanding how teams intend to control the flow of the game. Strategic analysis unveils the chess pieces on the board, revealing the initial moves in the unfolding narrative.

Example: *"As we kick off, notice the compact 4-3-3 formation from the home team. This suggests an emphasis on width and ball possession, setting the tone for their attacking strategy."*

Every player is a chess piece in motion, contributing to the strategic tapestry of the game. Play-by-play commentary involves tracking the movement and positioning of players, deciphering their roles within the team's strategy. Analyzing how players navigate the pitch provides valuable insights into offensive patterns, defensive structures, and the overall tactical approach.

Example: *"Watch the midfielder's intelligent movement here. By dropping deeper, they're creating an overload in the build-up, offering passing options and disrupting the opponent's defensive shape."*

Set-piece situations are strategic moments that can shift the balance of a match. Play-by-play commentary delves into the intricacies of set-piece strategies, whether it's a corner kick, free-kick, or penalty. Analyzing how teams position players, exploit vulnerabilities, and execute set-piece routines adds a layer of strategic depth to the commentary.

Example: *"This free-kick just outside the box presents a golden opportunity. Keep an eye on how they've set up—will they go for a direct shot or opt for a clever training ground routine?"*

Football is a dynamic game, and teams often make tactical adjustments based on the ebb and flow of play. Strategic analysis in play-by-play commentary involves unraveling these adjustments in real-time, providing viewers with insights into how teams respond to challenges, exploit weaknesses, and adapt their strategies to gain a competitive edge.

Example: "*A substitution in the 65th minute indicates a tactical shift. The introduction of an attacking midfielder suggests a more aggressive approach, as they seek to break down the opponent's resolute defense.*"

The defensive aspect of the game is a chess match in its own right. Strategic analysis delves into how teams shape up defensively, whether they opt for a high press, zonal marking, or a more conservative approach. Understanding defensive strategies enhances the appreciation for the cat-and-mouse game between attackers and defenders.

Example: "*Notice the organized defensive shape, with the full-backs tucking in and the midfield forming a compact block. This disciplined approach aims to nullify spaces and frustrate the opponent's attacking efforts.*"

Strategic analysis extends to individual performances within the team framework. Commentary goes beyond acknowledging goals and assists to contextualize how individual players contribute strategically. Recognizing the synergy between individual brilliance and collective strategy adds depth to the narrative.

Example: *"The striker's movement off the ball has been exceptional today. By pulling defenders out of position, they create spaces for teammates, adding a strategic dimension to their overall impact."*

Strategic analysis in play-by-play commentary is the lens through which the beautiful game reveals its tactical intricacies. As you listen to the next match, may the commentary unfold not just as a narration of events but as a strategic guide, decoding the chessboard of football with every word.

DECODING ON-FIELD TACTICS

At the heart of on-field tactics lies the formation—a blueprint that dictates the positioning of players on the pitch. Decoding formations involves recognizing the numerical sequence that defines a team's structure. Whether it's a classic 4-3-3, a resilient 5-4-1, or an adventurous 3-5-2, understanding these formations unveils the initial moves in the chess game of football strategy.

Example: "*The home team lines up in a flexible 4-2-3-1 formation. Notice the emphasis on a double pivot in midfield, offering both defensive stability and creative outlets.*"

On-field tactics are a symphony of orchestrated movements, particularly in the attacking phase. Decoding offensive patterns involves recognizing how teams build up play, create goal-scoring opportunities, and exploit spaces. Whether it's intricate passing sequences, wing-focused attacks, or direct long balls, understanding offensive patterns provides insights into a team's strategic intent.

Example: "*Watch as the wingers make diagonal runs, creating overloads on the flanks. This offensive pattern stretches the opposition and opens up channels for incisive passes into the final third.*"

A solid defense is the foundation of strategic prowess. Decoding defensive structures involves assessing how teams organize themselves to thwart opponent attacks. Whether it's high pressing, zonal marking, or a deep-lying block, understanding defensive structures provides valuable insights into a team's resilience and adaptability.

Example: "*The away side opts for a disciplined zonal marking approach. Notice how the defensive line maintains a compact shape, denying spaces for the opposition to exploit.*"

Football is a game of transitions—swift shifts between attack and defense. Decoding transition moments involves recognizing how teams react when possession is won or lost. Whether it's a quick counter-attack, a controlled build-up, or an immediate press to regain possession, understanding transition moments unveils the dynamism that defines modern football tactics.

Example: *"In this rapid transition, the midfielder intercepts the ball and initiates a lightning-quick counter. The speed of transition catches the opposition off guard, showcasing the tactical intelligence of the team."*

Every player is a strategic piece in the puzzle of on-field tactics. Decoding player roles involves recognizing the unique responsibilities assigned to each position. Whether it's the playmaking duties of a central midfielder, the defensive prowess of a full-back, or the goal-scoring instincts of a striker, understanding player roles adds depth to tactical analysis.

Example: *"The attacking midfielder drops deeper to link play, acting as the creative hub. This strategic movement allows the team to transition smoothly from defense to attack."*

Behind every on-field tactical decision is the influence of the manager. Decoding managerial strategies involves understanding the philosophies, preferences, and adaptability of the coach.

Whether it's a manager known for possession-based football, pressing tactics, or strategic flexibility, recognizing managerial influence adds another layer to the tactical narrative.

Example: *"The team's high defensive line and emphasis on ball retention reflect the manager's commitment to an attacking brand of football. The tactical identity mirrors the coach's strategic philosophy."*

Decoding on-field tactics is a journey that unveils the intricate strategies woven into the fabric of football. As you watch the next match, may your understanding of the tactical code enhance your appreciation for the chess game unfolding on the pitch—a game where every move is a strategic choice, and every decision shapes the destiny of the beautiful game.

EFFECTIVE USE OF STATISTICS AND ANALYTICS

Football analytics has undergone a transformative evolution, becoming an indispensable aspect of the sport. From simple match statistics to complex performance analytics, the data-driven revolution has changed how we perceive, analyze, and strategize in football. Understanding this evolution is the first step towards unlocking the true potential of statistics in the game.

Example: "*What began as a collection of basic statistics has evolved into a sophisticated system of analytics, providing a nuanced understanding of player performances, team dynamics, and strategic insights.*"

Effective use of statistics begins with dissecting player performances beyond goals and assists. Metrics such as Expected Goals (xG), pass completion rates, defensive contributions, and heat maps offer a granular view of a player's impact on the pitch.

These metrics help in evaluating individual strengths, identifying areas for improvement, and making informed decisions regarding player selection and tactics.

Example: "*Beyond the goal tally, assessing a striker's Expected Goals reveals the quality of chances created and the player's finishing proficiency, offering a deeper understanding of their overall contribution.*"

At the team level, statistical analysis unveils the dynamics of collective performance. Metrics like possession percentages, successful passes, and shot conversion rates provide insights into a team's playing style, strengths, and weaknesses. Effective use of team-level analytics empowers coaches to tailor strategies, optimize formations, and enhance overall tactical efficiency.

Example: "*A high possession percentage may indicate a team's emphasis on controlling the game, but it's the successful pass rates and shot conversion metrics that complete the narrative, revealing the effectiveness of their attacking prowess.*"

Advanced metrics go beyond the basics, offering tactical insights that shape strategic decisions. Metrics like Expected Assists (xA), pressing intensity, and distance covered provide a nuanced understanding of the tactical nuances that define a team's approach. Coaches and analysts leverage these advanced metrics to refine game plans, make halftime adjustments, and gain a competitive edge.

Example: "*Examining a team's pressing intensity through metrics reveals not just defensive capabilities but also the strategic emphasis on disrupting opponent build-ups and winning the ball higher up the pitch.*"

Statistics and analytics extend their reach to player health and physical conditioning. Monitoring metrics related to player workload, distance covered, and sprinting patterns helps in injury prevention and optimizing physical performance. Clubs utilize sports science analytics to tailor training regimens, manage player fatigue, and maximize overall fitness levels.

Example: "*By analyzing player workload metrics, teams can identify potential fatigue risks and tailor training programs to ensure peak physical condition, minimizing the chances of injuries and enhancing player longevity.*"

Effective use of statistics is a game-changer in scouting and recruitment. Analytics aid in identifying talent, assessing player suitability for specific positions, and predicting future success. Clubs leverage data-driven insights to make informed decisions in the transfer market, ensuring that recruitment strategies align with the team's tactical requirements and long-term objectives.

Example: "*Scouting analytics not only assess a player's current performance but also project their potential impact within a specific tactical system, enabling clubs to make strategic signings that align with their overall vision.*"

The effective use of statistics and analytics in football goes beyond mere numbers—it's about extracting meaningful insights, shaping strategies, and elevating the understanding of the game.

As you delve into the next match, may your appreciation for the beauty of football be enriched by the intricate narratives hidden within the data.

CHAPTER SIX

NAVIGATING UNPREDICTABLE MOMENTS

Football's allure lies in its unpredictability. No matter how meticulously a team plans, unexpected moments can shape the course of a match. Whether it's a last-minute goal, a spectacular save, or an unforeseen tactical shift, embracing the essence of unpredictability adds a layer of excitement that makes each match a unique narrative.

Example: "*In the grand theater of football, it's the unpredictable moments—the underdog's upset, the late-game heroics—that etch the stories we remember long after the final whistle.*

Matches are dynamic, and momentum swings are inevitable. Navigating unpredictable moments involves recognizing and adapting to shifts in momentum. Whether a team gains momentum through a quick succession of passes or a sudden change in tactics, understanding how to ride the waves of momentum can turn the tide in a team's favor.

Example: "*The opposing team has gained momentum with a series of quick attacks. Navigating this moment requires our team to regroup defensively and find opportunities to counter, disrupting their flow.*"

Unpredictable moments often call for tactical flexibility. Coaches who can make quick, informed decisions to adjust formations, roles, or strategies based on the unfolding chaos showcase a mastery of the game. Navigating unpredictable situations requires a willingness to deviate from the original game plan and adapt to the evolving dynamics on the pitch.

Example: "*Facing unexpected high pressing, the coach's tactical flexibility shines through as they make a substitution to reinforce the midfield, adjusting the team's shape to regain control.*"

Pressure situations are breeding grounds for unpredictability. Navigating these moments successfully involves maintaining composure under pressure.

Whether it's a goalkeeper making a crucial save, a defender clearing the ball off the line, or a forward staying composed in a one-on-one situation, moments of chaos require players to keep their cool and make rational decisions.

Example: "*In the dying minutes, with the score level, the striker maintains composure under pressure, calmly slotting the ball into the net. Navigating chaos with a clear mind is the mark of a seasoned player.*"

While unpredictable moments can pose challenges, they can also be leveraged as assets. Teams and players who embrace the unexpected, turning chaos into opportunities, often find success. Navigating unpredictability involves seeing beyond the immediate challenge and recognizing openings for creativity, innovation, and game-changing moments.

Example: "*A quick, unexpected change in formation catches the opponent off guard. Embracing the unpredictability, the team capitalizes on the confusion, creating space for a decisive counter-attack.*"

Unpredictable moments in football not only captivate players and coaches but also engage fans in a rollercoaster of emotions. Navigating these moments as a fan involves embracing the beauty of uncertainty, savoring the unpredictability that makes each match a captivating spectacle. The shared experience of navigating the chaos binds fans together in the collective journey of football fandom.

Example: " *supporters worldwide.*" *As fans, we celebrate the unpredictability of the game—the unexpected goals, the stunning comebacks. Navigating these moments together creates a sense of camaraderie among*

Navigating unpredictable moments in football is an inherent part of the sport's magic. As you watch the next match, may you find joy in the twists and turns, appreciating the beauty that emerges when chaos and order collide on the pitch.

HANDLING LIVE EVENTS AND UNEXPECTED TWISTS

Live events have a heartbeat of their own, a rhythm that refuses to conform to preconceived notions. Embracing the unpredictable nature of live events is the first step to handling unexpected twists with grace. Recognize that imperfections and spontaneity contribute to the unique charm of live experiences.

Example: "*In the theater of live events, the beauty lies in the unscripted moments—the unplanned laughter, the impromptu interactions, and the unexpected surprises that make each event memorable.*"

While spontaneity is celebrated, a solid foundation of preparation forms the backbone of successful live events. Anticipating potential challenges, having contingency plans, and ensuring technical readiness provide a safety net when unexpected twists occur. A well-prepared host or organizer can navigate surprises with confidence.

Example: "*Even in the most spontaneous of events, meticulous preparation ensures that technical glitches are swiftly addressed, unexpected delays are managed seamlessly, and the show goes on.*"

Live events demand quick thinking and adaptability. When faced with unexpected twists, the ability to pivot gracefully, make on-the-spot decisions, and adjust plans in real-time is invaluable. Embrace the dynamic nature of live events, turning challenges into opportunities for creative solutions.

Example: "*A sudden change in the schedule requires quick thinking. The host adapts by engaging the audience with an impromptu Q&A session, turning the unexpected delay into an interactive moment.*"

Live events thrive on audience engagement, even in the face of unexpected surprises. Whether it's technical difficulties, unforeseen changes, or impromptu elements, keeping the audience informed and involved ensures a shared experience. Transparent communication and a sense of humor can turn unexpected twists into shared moments of camaraderie.

Example: "*Applauding the audience for their patience during a technical glitch not only acknowledges the hiccup but also turns it into a collective experience, fostering a sense of community among attendees.*"

The live environment can be pressure-filled, especially when unexpected twists unfold. Maintaining composure under pressure is a hallmark of adept event organizers, hosts, and participants. Whether it's a sudden change in the program or an unforeseen challenge, a calm and collected demeanor sets the tone for a confident resolution.

Example: "*As the unexpected weather change forces an outdoor event indoors, the event coordinator maintains composure, assuring attendees and swiftly rearranging logistics for a seamless transition.*"

Unexpected twists are learning opportunities. After each live event, take time to evaluate the unexpected elements, identify areas for improvement, and incorporate lessons into future plans. The ability to learn and evolve from surprises contributes to continuous growth in handling live events with finesse.

Example: "*Post-event feedback and analysis reveal that an impromptu audience interaction segment was a highlight. Learning from this, future events incorporate more interactive elements to enhance audience engagement.*"

Handling live events and unexpected twists with grace is an art that blends preparation, adaptability, and a positive outlook. As you embark on the next live experience, may you find joy in the spontaneity, resilience in the face of surprises, and a sense of accomplishment in navigating the unscripted journey of live events.

ADAPTING TO CHANGES IN MOMENTUM

Momentum is a force that propels us forward or pulls us back, and its shifts are an inherent part of any journey. Acknowledging the dynamics of momentum involves recognizing that highs and lows are inevitable. Understanding that momentum is a fluctuating entity sets the stage for adapting to its changing currents.

Example: "Just as in a sports match, where the ebb and flow of momentum is constant, life too presents moments of exhilarating highs and challenging lows. Acknowledging this dynamic nature is the first step to effective adaptation."

When momentum takes an unexpected turn, maintaining calm amidst the storm is crucial. Whether it's a sudden surge of success or a challenging setback, a composed mindset allows for rational decision-making. Staying calm provides the clarity needed to assess the situation and adapt with grace.

Example: "*A team facing a sudden downturn in momentum maintains composure. Instead of panicking, they regroup, analyze the situation, and adapt their strategy, demonstrating that a calm demeanor is the antidote to turbulence.*"

Adapting to changes in momentum requires a flexible approach. Just as a skilled athlete adjusts their tactics based on the evolving dynamics of a match, embracing flexibility in our approach allows for responsive and strategic decision-making. A rigid mindset can be a hindrance, while flexibility opens doors to new possibilities.

Example: "*In the face of unexpected challenges, a professional who embraces flexibility reassesses their approach. By considering alternative solutions and adjusting their course, they turn adversity into an opportunity for growth.*"

Every shift in momentum carries lessons. Whether it's a period of success or a setback, extracting insights from these moments contributes to personal and professional growth.

Learning from momentum shifts involves introspection, identifying patterns, and understanding the factors that influence change. These lessons become valuable tools for future adaptation.

Example: "*After a successful project, taking the time to reflect on the contributing factors allows for a deeper understanding of what worked. Similarly, analyzing setbacks provides insights that inform a more resilient and informed approach moving forward.*"

Resilience is the bedrock of effective adaptation. Developing a resilient mindset involves viewing challenges as opportunities for learning and growth. Resilience enables individuals and teams to bounce back from setbacks, navigate uncertainties, and face changes in momentum with an unwavering spirit.

Example: "*A resilient individual, facing a career setback, channels the experience into a catalyst for personal development. The setback becomes a stepping stone towards a more resilient and adaptable professional journey.*"

Adapting to changes in momentum is not a solo endeavor. Collaboration and seeking support from others amplify our capacity for adaptation. Whether it's a team coming together during a challenging match or individuals leaning on their network during professional transitions, shared efforts and collective wisdom enhance the ability to navigate momentum shifts.

Example: "*In a project facing unexpected hurdles, a collaborative effort brings diverse perspectives to the table. The collective strength of the team becomes the driving force in adapting strategies and overcoming challenges.*"

The art of adapting to changes in momentum is a dynamic dance between acknowledgment, resilience, and flexibility. As you journey through the unpredictable currents of life, may the ability to ride the waves with grace become your guiding force, turning every change in momentum into an opportunity for growth and success.

CHAPTER SEVEN

ENGAGING WITH YOUR AUDIENCE

Engaging with your audience begins with authenticity—the genuine expression of your thoughts, values, and personality. Authenticity builds trust and resonates with your audience on a human level. When you bring your true self to the forefront, you invite others to do the same, fostering a connection based on transparency and sincerity.

Example: "*In a world saturated with curated content, authenticity stands out. When I share my experiences, successes, and challenges openly, it creates a relatable connection with my audience.*"

Effective engagement requires a deep understanding of your audience—their preferences, interests, and needs. Take the time to listen, observe, and learn about the individuals who make up your audience. Tailoring your communication to align with their expectations establishes a connection that goes beyond surface-level interaction.

Example: "*By actively listening to feedback and analyzing audience data, I discovered the specific topics my audience resonates with.* Understanding their preferences allows me to create content that speaks directly to their interests."

Engagement is a dialogue, not a monologue. Encourage two-way communication by inviting feedback, responding to comments, and actively participating in conversations. The exchange of ideas fosters a sense of community and involvement, transforming passive observers into active contributors to the narrative you're building.

Example: "*Rather than just sharing updates, I initiate discussions and ask questions. The comments section has become a space for a vibrant exchange of ideas, and the sense of community has grown organically.*"

Consistency is the backbone of sustained engagement. Regularly share content, updates, and responses to keep the connection alive. Additionally, timely interaction demonstrates your commitment to the relationship.

Whether it's acknowledging comments promptly or providing timely updates, consistent and timely engagement strengthens the bond with your audience.

Example: "*I set a regular posting schedule and make it a point to respond to comments within a reasonable time frame. This consistent and timely interaction has contributed to a sense of reliability and trust.*"

Beyond the content itself, showcasing your personality and passion adds depth to your engagement. Let your enthusiasm shine through, whether it's through your writing style, video presentations, or social media presence. Passion is contagious, and when your audience senses your genuine excitement, it becomes a magnet for connection.

Example: "*In my presentations, I infuse anecdotes that highlight my personal connection to the topic. Sharing my passion not only makes the content more engaging but also invites my audience to share their own experiences.*"

Feedback is a valuable compass for navigating the journey of engagement.

Embrace constructive criticism, celebrate positive feedback, and be open to evolving based on the insights gained. Adapting your approach according to audience feedback demonstrates a commitment to continuous improvement and a genuine desire to meet your audience's expectations.

Example: "*After receiving feedback about the desire for more in-depth tutorials, I adjusted my content strategy. The evolution based on audience input has led to a more enriching experience for both me and my audience.*"

Engaging with your audience is an art that weaves together authenticity, understanding, and continuous interaction. As you embark on your own journey of connection, may the threads of genuine communication create a tapestry of meaningful relationships, turning your audience into not just observers but active participants in the story you're unfolding.

UTILIZING SOCIAL MEDIA AND INTERACTIVE PLATFORMS

Your digital persona is more than just a profile picture and a bio. It's an extension of your authentic self. When utilizing social media, embrace transparency and showcase the real you. Share your passions, experiences, and even the occasional behind-the-scenes glimpses. Authenticity lays the foundation for genuine connections.

Example: "*Rather than projecting an idealized version of my life, I share both triumphs and challenges. This authenticity has resonated with my audience, creating a more meaningful and relatable digital presence.*"

Understanding your audience is paramount in crafting content that resonates. Utilize analytics tools to identify the demographics, preferences, and behaviors of your audience. Tailor your content to meet their expectations, addressing their interests, and sparking conversations that matter to them.

Example: *"By analyzing the analytics, I discovered that a significant portion of my audience is interested in a specific niche. This insight has guided my content creation, ensuring that it aligns with their expectations and preferences."*

Social media is not a one-sided broadcast—it's a conversation. Actively engage with your audience by responding to comments, asking questions, and participating in discussions. Create polls, host Q&A sessions, and acknowledge your audience's contributions. Fostering two-way communication transforms your platform into a dynamic space for interaction.

Example: *"Instead of just posting updates, I initiate conversations by asking for opinions, feedback, or even sharing personal anecdotes. This approach has turned my social media profiles into vibrant hubs of interactive dialogue."*

Explore and make the most of the interactive features offered by social media platforms.

From Instagram Stories polls to Twitter threads and live video sessions, these features provide dynamic ways to engage with your audience. Experiment with these tools to create a multi-dimensional and interactive digital experience.

Example: "*Hosting live Q&A sessions has allowed me to connect with my audience in real-time. The interactive element brings an immediacy that fosters a sense of community and connection.*"

Visuals are a powerful storytelling tool on social media. Whether it's eye-catching graphics, compelling videos, or well-curated photo albums, visual content captures attention and communicates narratives effectively. Utilize multimedia to convey your message, share experiences, and create a visually engaging feed.

Example: "*I've incorporated visual storytelling by using infographics to simplify complex concepts. The visual appeal not only attracts attention but also enhances the understanding and retention of the information.*"

Consistency is key in maintaining an active and engaged audience. Develop a posting schedule that aligns with your audience's habits and preferences. Additionally, strategize your content to ensure a balance between informative, entertaining, and thought-provoking posts. A thoughtful posting strategy keeps your audience anticipating and looking forward to your content.

Example: "*By posting consistently on specific days and times, I've noticed increased engagement. Understanding the peak hours when my audience is online has allowed me to strategically share content for optimal reach.*"

The world of social media and interactive platforms offers a dynamic canvas for digital expression. As you embark on this journey, may your online presence be more than just a scroll—it should be an immersive experience that fosters connections, cultivates community, and amplifies your authentic voice in the digital landscape.

CONNECTING WITH DIVERSE FAN BASES

To connect with a diverse fan base, celebrate diversity in your content. Showcase a range of perspectives, cultural references, and experiences. By weaving a rich tapestry of content that reflects various backgrounds, you create an inclusive space where fans from different walks of life can find elements that resonate with them.

Example: *"In my creative projects, I intentionally incorporate characters, narratives, and themes that reflect diverse cultures. This inclusivity not only broadens the appeal of my content but also fosters a sense of representation among diverse fan bases."*

Actively engage in cross-cultural conversations to bridge gaps and build understanding. Encourage fans to share their experiences, traditions, and viewpoints. By fostering a dialogue that transcends cultural barriers, you create a community where diverse voices are not only heard but celebrated.

Example: "*Hosting virtual meet-ups with fans from different parts of the world has opened up enlightening conversations. These exchanges not only enrich my understanding but also create a shared space where fans connect over common interests.*"

Tailor your engagement strategies to resonate with local cultures and customs. Whether it's adapting language, incorporating regional references, or acknowledging local festivities, personalizing your approach demonstrates a genuine effort to connect with diverse fan bases on their terms.

Example: "*During cultural festivals or holidays, I create themed content that reflects the celebratory spirit. This localized approach resonates with fans, fostering a sense of connection and shared celebration.*"

Collaboration knows no borders. Seek opportunities to collaborate with individuals or entities from different cultural backgrounds. Joint projects and partnerships not only introduce your content to new audiences but also create a synergy that celebrates the diversity inherent in shared endeavors.

Example: "*Collaborating with creators from different countries has been a transformative experience. Our joint projects bring together a fusion of cultural influences, creating content that speaks to a broader, international audience.*"

Navigating diverse fan bases requires a nuanced understanding of cultural sensitivity. Be mindful of cultural nuances, avoid stereotypes, and approach topics with respect. A commitment to cultural sensitivity fosters an environment where fans feel acknowledged and valued.

Example: "*In my online community, we have established guidelines that prioritize respectful conversations. This commitment to cultural sensitivity ensures that discussions remain inclusive and welcoming to fans from all backgrounds.*"

Actively amplify underrepresented voices within your fan base. Create opportunities for fans from marginalized communities to share their stories, perspectives, and contributions. By shining a spotlight on underrepresented voices, you contribute to a more inclusive and equitable fan community.

Example: "*In fan-created content showcases, I intentionally feature works from underrepresented creators. This not only amplifies their voices but also contributes to a more diverse and vibrant expression of fandom.*"

Connecting with diverse fan bases is an ongoing journey of inclusion, understanding, and celebration. As you navigate the landscape of fandom, may your efforts to connect resonate across borders, creating a tapestry of shared passion that transcends cultural differences and unites fans from every corner of the globe.

CHAPTER EIGHT

ETHICAL CONSIDERATIONS IN COMMENTARY

At the heart of ethical commentary lies a commitment to truth and accuracy. Whether analyzing a sports event, societal issues, or cultural phenomena, strive for factual integrity. Verify information before sharing, and be transparent about the sources that inform your commentary. Truth forms the bedrock upon which ethical expression stands.

Example: *"In my commentary, I prioritize fact-checking and thorough research. This commitment to truth not only builds credibility but also fosters a responsible and trustworthy dialogue with my audience."*

Ethical commentary embraces the richness of diverse perspectives. Acknowledge that opinions vary, and foster an environment where dissenting views are respected. Engage in constructive dialogue that encourages understanding rather than stifling diversity of thought. Respect becomes the bridge that connects disparate viewpoints.

Example: *"While expressing my viewpoint, I welcome differing opinions from my audience. Constructive debates not only enrich the conversation but also contribute to a more nuanced understanding of the topic at hand."*

Cultural sensitivity is an ethical cornerstone in commentary. Be attuned to the cultural context surrounding your commentary topics. Avoid perpetuating stereotypes, and approach subjects with an awareness of their cultural implications. By navigating conversations with cultural sensitivity, you contribute to an inclusive and respectful discourse.

Example: *"When discussing cultural practices or events, I take care to research and understand the context. This ensures that my commentary is nuanced, respectful, and free from inadvertent cultural insensitivity."*

The words we choose carry weight, and ethical commentary demands responsible language usage. Avoid inflammatory language, derogatory terms, or anything that may perpetuate harm.

Foster a space where language uplifts, educates, and promotes positive dialogue.

Example: "*In my commentary, I consciously choose words that promote understanding rather than incite discord. Responsible language usage is not just a commitment but a responsibility towards fostering a healthy discourse.*"

Transparency is a hallmark of ethical commentary, especially when it comes to relationships and affiliations. Disclose any potential conflicts of interest, sponsorships, or connections that might influence your commentary. This transparency builds trust and allows your audience to evaluate your commentary in the appropriate context.

Example: "*If I have affiliations with entities mentioned in my commentary, I make it clear to my audience. Transparency ensures that my viewers are aware of any potential biases and can form their judgments accordingly.*"

Sensitive topics demand a thoughtful approach.

When commenting on issues that may be emotionally charged or trigger strong reactions, exercise empathy and consider the potential impact of your words. Ethical commentary involves recognizing the responsibility that comes with addressing sensitive subjects.

Example: "*In discussing mental health, I approach the topic with empathy and provide resources for support. Ethical engagement with sensitive topics goes beyond commentary; it's about contributing positively to the well-being of my audience.*"

Ethical considerations in commentary are not constraints but guiding principles that elevate discourse. As you navigate the realms of expression, may your commentary be a beacon of ethical awareness, fostering a space where words contribute positively to understanding, respect, and the shared pursuit of knowledge.

MAINTAINING FAIRNESS AND AVOIDING BIAS

Maintaining fairness begins with a steadfast commitment to objectivity. Strive to present information in a balanced manner, acknowledging multiple sides of an issue. Objectivity fosters a space where diverse viewpoints can coexist and encourages critical thinking among your audience.

Example: "*In my commentary, I consciously present different perspectives on a topic, allowing my audience to form their opinions. This commitment to objectivity ensures that the discourse remains open and inclusive.*"

Unconscious biases can seep into commentary, influencing perspectives unintentionally. Recognize and confront your implicit biases by actively reflecting on your own preconceptions. This self-awareness is a powerful tool for fostering fairness, as it allows you to approach topics with a more conscious and impartial mindset.

Example: "*I make a conscious effort to reflect on my own biases before delving into a topic. This reflective practice helps me identify potential biases and ensures that my commentary is grounded in fairness.*"

To mitigate bias, diversify your sources and perspectives. Seek information from a range of outlets, experts, and voices. This not only broadens your own understanding but also ensures that your commentary reflects a mosaic of viewpoints, reducing the risk of unintentional bias.

Example: "*In preparing for my commentary, I consult a variety of sources with differing perspectives. This multifaceted approach not only enriches my own understanding but also contributes to a more well-rounded and fair narrative.*"

Guard against perpetuating stereotypes or making sweeping generalizations. Recognize the diversity within groups and communities, and avoid reducing individuals to clichéd narratives. Steering clear of stereotypes contributes to fair and nuanced commentary that respects the complexity of human experiences.

Example: "*In discussing cultural topics, I avoid relying on stereotypes and instead focus on individual stories and experiences. This approach ensures that my commentary remains respectful and free from generalized assumptions.*"

Fair commentary embraces inclusivity by actively inviting diverse voices into the conversation. Feature guest contributors, collaborate with individuals from different backgrounds, and create a platform that amplifies underrepresented perspectives. This intentional inclusion fosters a richer and more equitable discourse.

Example: "*In my commentary series, I regularly invite guest contributors who bring unique perspectives to the table. This collaborative effort not only diversifies the narrative but also ensures that a multitude of voices is heard.*"

Open yourself to constructive criticism as a means of refining your commentary. Establish a feedback loop with your audience and be receptive to diverse viewpoints.

Embracing constructive criticism is not a sign of weakness but a testament to your commitment to continuous improvement and fairness.

Example: *"When my audience provides constructive criticism, I see it as an opportunity to learn and grow. This openness to feedback ensures that my commentary remains a dynamic and evolving space for diverse perspectives."*

Maintaining fairness and avoiding bias in commentary is a continual process of introspection, diversification, and active engagement. As you embark on this journey, may your commentary serve as a beacon of fairness, fostering a space where diverse voices are not just acknowledged but celebrated.

ADDRESSING CONTROVERSIAL TOPICS RESPONSIBLY

Before delving into a controversial topic, arm yourself with knowledge. Thorough research is the cornerstone of responsible commentary. Understand the nuances, historical context, and various perspectives surrounding the issue. This groundwork not only fortifies your arguments but also demonstrates a commitment to informed dialogue.

Example: "*In addressing a controversial topic, I dedicate ample time to research, ensuring that I grasp the intricacies involved. This commitment to understanding forms the basis for a responsible exploration of the subject.*"

Responsible commentary acknowledges that controversies are often multifaceted. Presenting multiple perspectives helps your audience see the complexity of the issue. Encourage critical thinking by showcasing differing viewpoints, fostering an environment where your audience can form their conclusions based on a comprehensive understanding.

Example: "*Rather than advocating for a singular stance, I present various perspectives on the controversial topic. This approach encourages my audience to engage critically and consider the nuances at play.*"

Language is a powerful tool that can either fuel or temper controversy. Choose your words with care, opting for clarity over sensationalism. Avoid inflammatory language that may escalate tensions, and strive for a tone that fosters respectful dialogue. Mindful language choices contribute to a discourse that is both impactful and responsible.

Example: "*When addressing a sensitive subject, I opt for language that is measured and respectful. This ensures that my commentary promotes understanding rather than inciting unnecessary discord.*"

Controversial topics often arise within broader contexts. Contextualizing the discussion helps your audience appreciate the interconnectedness of issues and promotes a more nuanced understanding.

Provide historical background, consider cultural influences, and highlight relevant factors that contribute to the complexity of the controversy.

Example: "*Before diving into the controversial aspect, I take the time to contextualize the discussion. This contextualization helps my audience grasp the broader picture and appreciate the intricacies involved.*"

Responsible commentary fosters an environment for constructive dialogue. Encourage your audience to share their opinions, engage with differing viewpoints, and participate in a respectful exchange of ideas. Actively moderate discussions to ensure that the conversation remains constructive rather than divisive.

Example: "*In the comment section, I actively encourage constructive dialogue. By setting a tone of respect and openness, I create a space where my audience feels comfortable expressing their opinions thoughtfully.*"

No commentary is exhaustive, especially on controversial topics. Acknowledge the limitations of your perspective and remain open to evolving viewpoints.

Be transparent about the complexities inherent in the issue, and demonstrate a willingness to adapt your understanding as new information emerges.

Example: "*I recognize that my perspective is not all-encompassing. In addressing a controversial topic, I acknowledge the limitations of my viewpoint and encourage my audience to contribute to an ongoing, evolving dialogue.*"

Addressing controversial topics responsibly is a delicate dance of knowledge, empathy, and ethical communication. As you navigate this terrain, may your commentary serve as a beacon of thoughtful exploration, contributing to a discourse that transcends controversy and paves the way for understanding and unity.

CONCLUSION

In the pages of "Commentary Playbook: Mastering the Art of Engaging Football Analysis," Angela Keen invites readers into the dynamic world of sports commentary, unraveling the intricacies of the craft with expertise and passion. As the author, Keen doesn't merely dissect the technical aspects of commentary; she acts as a seasoned guide, leading readers through the art of storytelling, strategic analysis, and the nuances of engaging football analysis.

The journey within this playbook is not a one-size-fits-all approach but a comprehensive exploration that accommodates both aspiring and seasoned commentators. Keen's meticulous breakdown of topics, from understanding the commentator's influence on viewer experience to the fine balance between scripting and improvisation, provides a roadmap for mastering the art of football analysis. With each chapter, the reader delves into the diverse facets of commentary, gaining insights that transcend the boundaries of the game itself.

What sets "Commentary Playbook" apart is its holistic approach. Keen doesn't just unravel the technicalities of delivering engaging commentary; she delves into the psychology of players, the dynamics of teamwork, and the ever-evolving landscape of sports media. Through practical advice, illustrative examples, and thought-provoking exercises, Keen empowers readers to not only analyze the game but to craft narratives that resonate with audiences, fostering a genuine connection between commentator and viewer.

The author's voice resonates with a profound love for the game, and her guidance extends beyond the theoretical into the realm of practical application. From decoding strategic plays to navigating the complexities of live events, Angela Keen seamlessly weaves her experiences into the narrative, offering a personal touch that transforms this playbook into more than just a guide—it becomes a mentorship in the art of football commentary.

As readers turn the final pages of "Commentary Playbook," they are not just equipped with technical prowess; they carry with them a deeper understanding of the stories that unfold on the football field. Angela Keen's playbook is an enduring resource, a compass for those embarking on a commentary career and a source of inspiration for those seeking to refine their craft. Through its pages, the reader not only learns about football analysis but is invited into the very soul of the game, where passion meets expertise in the pursuit of the perfect commentary. Angela Keen's "Commentary Playbook" is not just a guide; it's an immersive journey into the heart of football commentary, ensuring that each reader emerges not just as a commentator but as a storyteller who masterfully navigates the beautiful game.

Printed in Dunstable, United Kingdom

71194593R00070